Teach Someone to Roller Skate!

(Even Yourself!)

A Beginning Roller Skating Course for All Ages

Written and Illustrated by
Marty Donnellan
© 2013. All rights reserved.

ISBN 10   0-9791982-5-9
ISBN 13   978-0-9791982-5-0

Marturion, LLC
2870 Callie Still Road / Lawrenceville, GA 30045

Other Books by Marty Donnellan

Hannah Scrabble Cozy Mysteries

Mountain City Murder
Murder at the Company Picnic
Thursday Mystery

Frendibles Books

Henbit and Her Sisters
Book One of the Forest of the Frendibles

Tegera
Book Two of the Forest of the Frendibles

Henbit and the Roly Poly

Henbit and Maypop

Acknowledgements

Playland Skating Rink, Doraville, GA
Sparkles of Gwinnett, Grayson, GA
All American Skating Center, Stone Mtn., GA

Thanks to the owners and managers of these rinks
for providing places for me to skate since 1968!

⌘   ⌘   ⌘   ⌘

Table of Contents

Table of Contents (continued)

Hi, everyone! I love my job as a roller skating coach at area rinks. Over time I have taught scores of children and adults how to skate, and many others how to improve their skating. I've also watched many people struggle to skate on their own, or struggle to teach someone else.

I decided to write and illustrate this manual as a way to offer my tried and true methods to everyone: to people with no access to a professional coach, or people with time constraints, or people who simply like to do things themselves.

By studying my clear text and engaging illustrations, you can now teach anyone – even yourself or your child – how to skate correctly, with skill and enjoyment.

Below are a few of the topics we'll cover:

- Beginning skating positions and postures
- How to keep from falling, how to fall, and how to get up
- How to stop
- How to carve, pump, swizzle, and do crossovers
- Beginning backwards skating
- Special age groups such as older adults and preschoolers
- Beginning intermediate moves such as two-footed spins and the Mohawk turn

...and more! Roller skating definitely feels strange at first. But once you master the basics, it can be ridiculously fun, providing lifelong enjoyment, fitness and stress relief. You can take the sport in many different directions, including speed skating, artistic skating, rhythm and jam skating, roller hockey, derby and slalom. No matter how good you get, there are always new things to learn. So let's lace up and get started.

Marty Donnellan

Chapter One: Before You Skate

"What's the Difference Between Quad Skates and Inline Skates?"

A quad skate has four wheels oriented in a rectangular shape, two in front and two in back. An inline skate has between three and five wheels (usually four) lined up one behind the other. Whether you end up skating in quad skates or inline skates is a matter of preference. Your choice will depend on the kind of skating you decide you want to pursue, and your budget. All types of skates can do the same kinds of things. But some are better for jumping, and others are better for going fast. Some are better for intricate footwork, while others are better for going straight.

On the following page, we'll look at some other differences between quad and inline skates. (Wheels, boots and trucks are discussed in even greater detail on page 15.)

Quads Vs. Inlines: Wheels

The front wheel of the inline skate usually extends beyond the toe, while the front wheels of the quad skate line up under the ball of the foot. Inline wheels are narrower than quad wheels, without sharply defined edges. Inline skates require a bit more balancing ability.

Quads Vs. Inlines: Brakes

Quad skates usually have a stopper in the front, while inlines, except for speed skates, usually have a stopper in the back.

Quads Vs. Inlines: Boots

Quad skates have high or low leather or leather-type boots which are fitted close to the foot and ankle. Recreational inline skates have thicker and often taller boots made of foam filled fabric partially covered with a hard plastic shell. Speed inline skates have hard, low cut boots.

Quads Vs. Inlines: Trucks

All but the least expensive quad skates have trucks which are adjustable. Adjustable trucks allow varying degrees of give between the axles and the plate. This movement gives the skater greater maneuverability. Inline skates do not have trucks. The frame is often one molded piece which extends from the wheels to close to the top of the boot. Maneuverability of the skate is accomplished in other ways.

Four Styles of Skates and Skaters

On the following pages we'll look at the four most common kinds of skates in use today: the recreational inline skate; the quad artistic skate (sometimes called the rhythm skate); the quad jam skate (similar in most ways to the derby skate); and the inline speed skate. Keep in mind that there are variations within each type of skate, such as higher vs. lower boots, larger vs. smaller wheels, higher vs. lower heels, hardness of wheels, etc.

There are other types of skates not covered in this book, such as aggressive inline skates, artistic inline skates, and all-terrain skates. Skates, and skating, continue to evolve.

Recreational Inline Skate

- Popular outdoors and in rinks
- Brake is in back
- No trucks
- Frame is one welded piece
- Casual, all-purpose skate

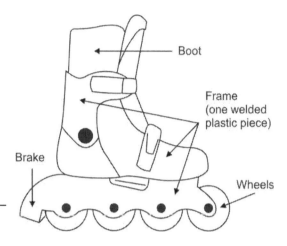

Our skater, Austin, is happy to demonstrate. Nothing fancy, he just likes to skate.

Artistic Quad Skate
(similar to Rhythm Quad Skate)

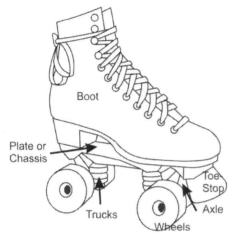

- Narrow wheels
- A higher heel which pushes the foot forward for spinning and jumping
- A high-topped boot
- A large toe stop which can be replaced with smaller "dance plugs"
- Adjustable trucks

To the right is how an artistic skater might look:

If you want to pursue artistic skating like Audrey, you'll need the grace of a ballerina and the strength of an athlete.

Jam Skate
(similar to Roller Derby Skate)

- A flat heel
- Unusually wide wheels for a broader base of support
- A softer, low-cut boot
- More lightweight than artistic skates
- Adjustable trucks
- Smaller toe-stops called jam plugs

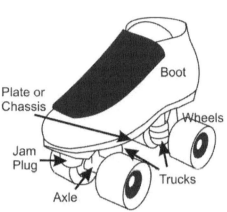

Showing off some footwork to the left is Clay, a jam skater. Later, he will impress and possibly alarm you with some of his break dancing moves.

If you want to jam skate, get used to skating on your toes and insteps. And doing flares and airchairs.

Inline Speed Skate

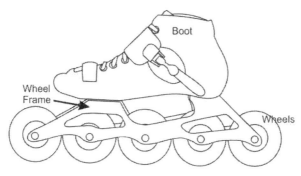

- Three to five extra large wheels which protrude farther in front and back than in recreational inlines, giving an advantage in fast, forward skating ■ No brakes
- Low-cut boot is a hard "shell" welded to frame

This is how a speed skater might look:

If you want to speed skate like Wimbledon Wimpleton III, get used to going really fast, having knees that can bend deeply, training many hours per week, and burning loads of calories.

"Should I Wear a Helmet and Padding?"

Good question. Speed and derby skaters are required to wear protective gear, but I don't know of any rink which requires this of ordinary patrons. **However, I believe that all beginning students should wear both.** If you are outside, skating on concrete or asphalt, you should definitely wear both. Sometimes, students tell me they don't want to look silly or wimpy, but the risk of injury while skating is very real. Rinks in many states have "skate at your own risk" policies supported by law. That's because even experienced professionals sometimes fall and get hurt.

Think about it – wearing protective padding could mean the difference between a nasty bruise and some soreness, and a broken bone or concussion. Not only that, but people who wear protective gear can feel less fearful about trying new things, because they know that if they do fall, there is lots of plastic and padding protecting them. Keep in mind that sometimes injuries occur even with protective gear. Ultimately, it's your decision.

"Should I Rent Skates or Buy Them?"

The rink's rental skates are fine to learn in, and you can even make a good deal of progress in them. But later on, if you plan on skating at least once a week, you may prefer to buy your own. That way, you'll know what to expect from your skates, and they will conform to your feet. Not only that, it's easy to replace or upgrade individual components – bearings, wheels, plates, boots and so on.

If you buy skates, choose the best you can possibly afford for your level of ability. (Hint: sporting goods stores don't sell many quad skates, and what they do sell are barely entry level.) Just like shoes, some brands of skates run a little wide and some a little narrow – some a little long and some a little short. Some have more padding inside than others. Some have metal versus plastic plates.

If you are thinking about buying skates for a young child, refer to the advice on page 24.

It helps to gather all the information you can about a variety of brands and styles. The rink pro shop is a great place to start. Talk to other skaters; join an internet discussion board for skaters; and "test drive" as many skates as possible.

If you buy skates, here are a few important things to remember:

New Skates: Wheels

The wheels on your new skates very likely have been tightened at the factory so that they don't spin freely enough. You may need to loosen them.

In time, you may wish to upgrade the wheels. The wheels your skates come with are not always the best. Then there is the degree of wheel hardness, called the *durometer*. Hardness is the wheels' ability to grip a given skate surface, and has a lot to do with your skating enjoyment. Wheels range from a durometer of 72a to 103a or more, with 72a being a soft, grippy outdoor wheel suitable for hockey, and 103a being a hard, slippery indoor wheel good for dancing. Indoor wheels usually start at around 84a. A too soft wheel will feel sluggish on an indoor concrete or wood floor. A too hard wheel will result in too little control for your level of ability. Durometer selection is also affected by the skater's weight and the temperature. It's ultimately a matter of preference gained over time. Even skaters with the same skates doing the same things with them might swear by different wheels.

Another factor to consider is the width of the wheel. Jamskaters often prefer very wide wheels, while figure skaters usually favor narrower wheels.

New Skates: Boots

The boots of your new skates will likely need some breaking in. It can take up to ten sessions for you to feel fully comfortable in them.

New Skates: Trucks

The trucks of your new skates have been factory set to maximum tightness, allowing the axles no movement. This is for your safety. As you progress in skill, you may want to begin gradually loosening the trucks. Having looser trucks will give you more maneuverability.

Troubleshooting Rental Skates

Say you've decided you want to stick with rental skates for awhile. That's fine, but they can be unpredictable. Some rinks maintain their skates better than other rinks. Some have multiple styles to choose from.

Be sure and inspect your rentals every time you put them on. Check the wheels. Are they so tightly fastened that they barely roll? Ask the pro shop to loosen them. Are they so loose that you can hear a clacking noise as you move the wheel up and down on the axle? This can result in a dangerous loss of control; have them tightened. The wheels should all be tightened just enough to spin freely.

Another common problem is a skate that doesn't roll cleanly forward, but lists to one side or another. This probably means that the plate is misaligned. Don't hesitate to exchange the pair. In fact, feel free to exchange skates for any reason. You paid for the session and you deserve skates that will help you enjoy yourself, not seethe with frustration. If you do get a pair you like, remember the number on them so you can request them again.

Wear Skates that Fit

Whether you are wearing rental skates or your own, make sure they fit properly. They should fit like your shoes, snug but not too tight. Make sure there is a little extra room in the toe, and that your heel fits neatly into the boot. Lace or buckle the skates all the way to the top, securing lace ends away from axles and wheels. Make sure all of the wheels are spinning freely with no extra movement on the axle.

You should wear one well fitting pair of socks under your skates. If your skates give you blisters, mark the spot and apply duct tape to your skin before your next skate. Blisters can't form where there is no friction, and duct tape works even better than bandages to eliminate friction.

If your blisters are usually on your toes, it may not be the skate. You may be guilty of pushing off too frequently with your toes. Remember to push from the heel, not allowing the other skate to trail behind you.

The right pair of skates can greatly increase your enjoyment and mastery of the sport, while a substandard or ill-fitting pair can make you work harder than you need to, and even frustrate you to the point of wanting to give up.

Be Aware of Foot Problems

There are several foot abnormalities that can cause problems, not only in your skating but in other sports as well. First, make sure your skates fit well and are laced securely. Stand on the carpet and have someone look at your feet as you walk away. Whether you are wearing quads or inlines, your wheels should be centered directly under your legs and feet. If your ankles and feet are leaning outwards, they are said to be *pronating*. This is a fairly common problem, and is accompanied by low arches, or "flat feet". Another, less common, problem are feet that *supinate*. That is when ankles and feet lean inwards, and arches are unusually high. Because pronating feet are so much more common, we'll look only at them in the illustrations below.

Quad Skates As Seen From Behind

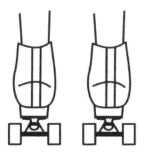 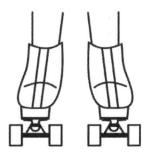

Proper stance – wheels are centered under feet. This means easy, effective skating. The wheels are doing their share of the work.

Poor stance – feet and ankles are pronating outward. This means hard work, wasted energy and not very effective skating.

Inline Skates As Seen From Behind

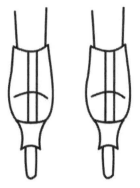

Proper stance – wheels are centered under feet. This means easy, effective skating. The wheels are doing their share of the work.

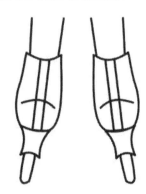

Poor stance – feet and ankles are pronating outward. This means hard work, wasted energy and not very effective skating.

If you are wearing inline skates, it's possible that your feet are fine but that the plates are incorrectly mounted off-center. Or, and more likely, you could have weak ankles which are not used to balancing above the inline skate's slim, linear base of support. In these cases, switching to quad skates, which have a broader, rectangular base of support, might help.

If your feet pronate or supinate, learn some strengthening exercises and/or experiment with orthotics in your skates to better position and support your feet. Skating without orthotics if you need them can put extra stress on your feet and legs, cause foot pain and shin splints, and increase the risk of sprains and fractures. Below is another chart showing these common foot problems.

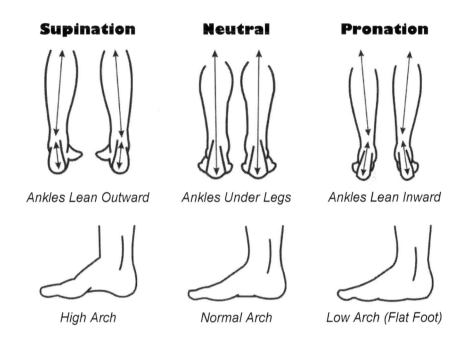

Supination	Neutral	Pronation
Ankles Lean Outward	Ankles Under Legs	Ankles Lean Inward
High Arch	Normal Arch	Low Arch (Flat Foot)

Two Exercises for Pronating or Supinating Feet

Toe Pickups: Put ten marbles on the floor. Your feet should be bare. Pick up one marble after another with your toes and put them in a cup. Do three repetitions for each foot.

Toe Rollups: Put a dishtowel on the floor. Roll it up with your toes. Then unroll it with your toes. Repeat ten times.

"I'm Over 45, Overweight and/or Out of Shape. Can I Learn to Skate?"

Of course you can. But you will need to proceed carefully. You may already know that you run a higher risk than other students of a catastrophic fall (a fall involving a fractured or broken bone). Your muscles are weaker; your feet are bearing more weight than they should; your bones are more brittle; and your "fear factor" is probably higher.

Many broken bones occur during the more vulnerable student's very first hour of skating. And the majority of these happen when the student falls backwards or sideways, directly onto the wrists, elbows, back, or head.

That's why I have developed a special method for introducing this student to skating. I call it the *Art of Skating Defensively.* Normally, the correct posture for beginning skating is **head over shoulders; shoulders over waist; waist over hips; and hips over feet – with back straight, knees bent and arms raised to about waist level.** I often tell students to imagine a pole coming from the sky and going vertically through their bodies and into the ground.

If you fall into the "vulnerable" category, however, your initial skating posture will be somewhat different. Later on, after your skating skills and confidence improve, you can transition to the normal posture. This could take anywhere from a week to a few months. Be patient and don't give up.

For now, your posture will somewhat resemble that of a boxer in defensive mode. Consider wearing a helmet, knee, elbow and wrist pads. Your back will be straight and your knees bent, but you should tilt your shoulders, neck and head slightly forward. Tuck your arms, elbows and loosely closed fists into your chest. This way, if you fall it will be forward, probably onto your knees – and your more fragile elbows, wrists, and the back of your head will be out of harm's way. Refer to the section on falling on page 34.

Let's look at Emilio, left, as he demonstrates the defensive posture. I admire Emilio, because, one, he's not afraid to start where he's at, which is the beginning, and, two, he's not too proud to take proper precautions. After a year of skating two or three times a week, Emilio is going to look a bit different.

A final point: if you are using skating as a beginning fitness program after years of "nothing", I strongly advise you to supplement it with regular walking, swimming, dance, or some other gentle sport that you enjoy.

"Can I Teach Someone Under Five to Skate?"

Sure you can. I have taught kids as young as three. It helps to remember how little people learn. Think "preschool" – bright, simple visuals, funny rhymes, games, shouted repetitions... and lots of smiles and encouragement.

With my youngest students, sometimes verbally explaining the four basic skating positions (discussed in the next section) simply doesn't work. Three of the positions have letter names, and some younger kids have not yet learned the alphabet. Demonstrating the position doesn't necessarily work, either – little eyes aren't always watching what I want them to – darn those disco balls overhead. When this is the case, I have them sit on the bench where I arrange their feet in the correct position. I have them look at their feet and feel the shape of their feet. I have them stand again, forming the position with their arms as well as feet. I call the name of the position and they shout it back to me.

I tell them that skating feet are different than walking feet. I show them a picture of "walking feet" versus "skating feet" (seen on the next page). Sometimes I use a rhyme, sung to the tune of "Twinkle, Twinkle, Little Star": *My knees are bent, my back is straight, my toes are out, now I can skate.* I have even been known to wear a pair of enormous red clown shoes to demonstrate the position. The clown shoes get their attention, though parents look at me a little strangely.

Feet That Walk
(Feet are parallel)

Feet That Skate
(Heels together, toes out)

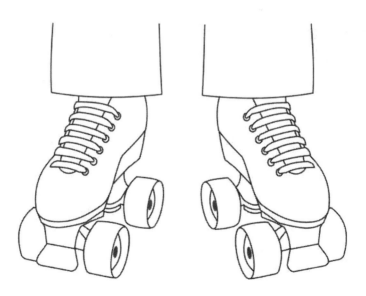

Preschoolers and Emotions

On the emotional front, one problem common among preschoolers is that they can quickly progress from happiness to frustration to tears, or even shutdown – that is, a stubborn refusal to do anything further – in thirty seconds or less. When I see trouble brewing, I bring out my large inflatable ball and ask who wants to play. No one has ever said "Not me" to this question. I begin by rolling the ball to the student. When she can catch it and roll it back without falling, we progress to bouncing and gently throwing the ball to each other. The more kids the merrier.

The ball totally takes the pressure off. The kids become so engrossed with rolling, throwing, bouncing, chasing and catching the ball that they forget they are learning to skate. I also sometimes use the ball with older students, because it's a great way to build agility and balance.

With young children, I recommend keeping lessons brief, to no longer than thirty minutes. Never pressure a young child to do more than her body is physically capable of doing at that point. Accept her level of mastery, with plenty of encouragement and praise. Make it fun.

Sometimes, to encourage a hesitant or upset child, I forget skating for a minute, and just start crawling around on the floor. The child quickly joins in, since that is something she knows she can do, plus it is silly. Before I know it, the child's funk has passed, her strong spirit has reasserted itself, and she is again attempting to skate.

Parent/Child Dynamics

If you are a parent trying to teach your preschooler to skate, let the parent/child dynamic work for you and not against you. In my classes, parents are welcome to join their young child on the floor. Many times the child benefits. But if the parent is tense, the child becomes tense, too. Also, some kids have an unfortunate tendency to turn into jelly when parents are assisting. Their legs go limp, they cling, the parents get more frustrated, the kids cling harder, and no one learns how to skate. I request that those parents sit down, or be available for emergency cuddling only, so the child won't be so distracted.

It's normal for parents to want their kids to succeed in front of others, but guys, try to relax. Allow your child to hold only one of your hands or fingers at first, and then have her let go. It's safer if you are not on skates while helping your child. Teaching your child to skate will require an extra dose of patience and calm on your part.

Skates for the Youngest Skaters

Not to disparage rental skates, but I have seen some younger children really struggle to learn in them. Sometimes, after a lesson or two, their parents buy them their own pair of skates. More often than not, their performance improves dramatically. This is because the boots provide more support, and the wheels don't spin so freely.

Entry level quad skates for children are not expensive. You can check your rink's pro shop, but Walmart and Target offer them for $20.00-$40.00. I love these kiddie skates. Many of them combine the best features of quads and inlines for maximum comfort and performance. They have a chassis and wheel setup like quad skates, and "fitness" boots like inlines, with a hard shell, fabric padding, and Velcro and clip closures. The wheels are hard plastic, their slipperiness offset by the fact that the wheels don't spin freely. For young kids, I would not loosen the wheels, but leave them as they are. I probably don't need to point out that these inexpensive children's skates do not have adjustable trucks.

If your child is using rentals and is not progressing as much you would like, but you're not yet ready to purchase skates, you can ask the rink to temporarily tighten the child's wheels, as discussed on page 42. This will at least get her used to being on skates.

If *none* of the above methods work and your child is under four, it might be time to throw in the towel temporarily and put her in those plastic play skates that rinks sometimes offer to the smallest skaters. These toy skates have a very broad, flat base of support and tiny wheels which hardly roll at all. I've never seen a child who could not get around in those things. Let your child have fun in the play skates and later she will graduate to the real thing.

Chapter Two: Basic Positions

Four Basic Skating Positions

Now it's time to learn some basic skating positions. Most of our illustrations from this point forward reference quad skates, but most of the same principles apply to inlines (a major exception being the angle of wheels to the floor when performing carves and crossovers). The diagram on the next page below shows your skates in a parallel position, that is, when they are on your feet and you are looking down at them. I call this parallel position "Piano Keys" because skates are close together, side by side and pointing straight ahead. You can use Piano Keys when you want to just roll along without stroking, but they won't help you skate – in fact, they'll mess you up. More on that later.

Be sure and check out the "Drills" section beginning on page 82. Drills are a fantastic way to reinforce each new skill.

Piano Keys (Parallel) Position

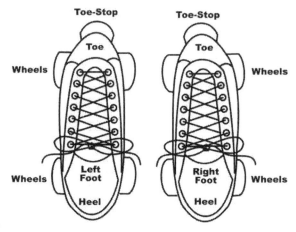

Good for rolling along but not for stroking...

Our second position, seen on the next page, is called the "T-Position". The T-Position is used in many ways. The first way we use it is to create stability on skates. I call this position the "Safety Lock".

To assume the Safety Lock Position, pick up your right foot and tuck the heel midway between the wheels of your left skate. All eight wheels should be squarely on the floor. Your skates should form a 90 degree angle, forming the shape of a sideways capital "T". Your right heel should be close to but not touching the side of your left skate. Now bend your knees a little. There. You will stay put.

T-Position (Safety Lock)

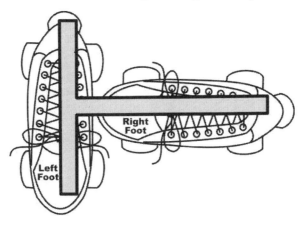

In the illustration at right, Celia demonstrates the Safety Lock Position. Even though her knees should bend a little more, she is stable and in no danger of falling. Her arms are extended a little but relaxed.

Later on, a modified T-position is used to create a powerful push-off, and can also be used to bring the skater to a stop.

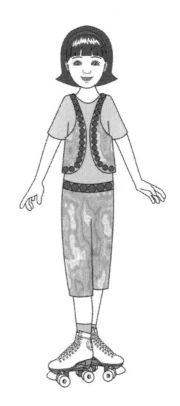

Our next position, seen below, is called the "V-Position". THIS IS THE POSITION USED FOR BASIC SKATING. Place your heels together with your toes out, in the shape of a "V". Your V-shape doesn't have to be wide. In fact, it should form no more than a 45 degree angle. Make sure your skates are not touching and that your knees are bent a little.

V-Position

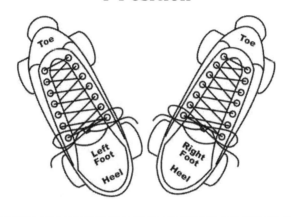

V-Position as Seen From the Front

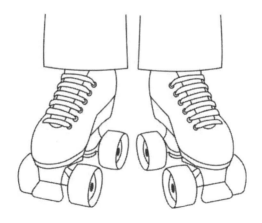

Awesome. Now practice the "Reverse V-Position", below. You'll use this position when you begin to skate backwards and in other moves. This time your toes will be together and your heels will be out. Again, don't let your skates touch and make sure your knees are bending.

Reverse V-Position

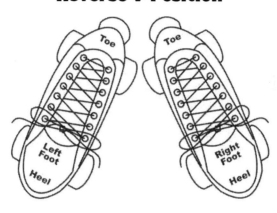

Reverse V-Position as Seen From the Front

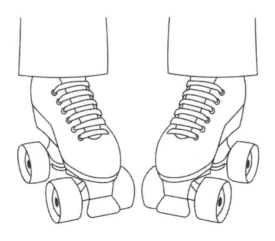

34

How to Keep From Falling

Oh dear, it's time to talk about falling. Every skater loses her balance. Here's what to do if you are skating along, like Ashanti in Figure A (below), and suddenly feel like you are losing your balance: relax your knees and drop your body a fourth of the way down (Figure B); extend your arms to each side for balance; stop trying to skate; and just roll. This is called a "Drop and Roll", and can help you regain your balance. If you *still* feel off balance, like Ashanti in Figure C, drop even lower, as far down as you can go. Hug your knees, assume a squatting position, and roll. If, after becoming a cannonball, you still fall... at least you won't have far to go.

Figure A   Figure B   Figure C

How to Fall as Safely as Possible

No skater wants to fall, but every skater does. That's why it's a good idea to learn how to fall and get up properly before attempting to skate. You can practice on or off skates. If you know a fall is coming, try to do what I call an "Eggroll". Bend your head forward and tuck in your elbows, like an egg (refer to Emilio on page 23). Let your knees buckle as you come to a sliding landing on your knees or, even better, your backside. Avoid falling directly on your elbows, wrists or, obviously, head. If you use your hands to brace your fall, make sure your fingers face outward, not inward. Then raise your hands so another skater can't roll over them and break a bone. Ashanti, below, demonstrates how to fall, with style.

How to Get Up After You Fall

This, too, can be practiced on or off skates.

Step One. After falling, Emily, above, gets on her hands and knees. You can tell young children to get on all fours like a puppy dog – "bark, bark!" *(Emily, get that gum out of your mouth! Gum on the skate floor can mess it up and also make people trip. If you fell while chewing gum, you could choke.)*

Step Two. Jamal, on the next page, has already gotten on his hands and knees like Emily. Now he rocks back on his heels, centering his arms and hands between his knees. You can tell young children to squat like a frog – "rivet!" See how Jamal's body weight is distributed evenly across both legs and feet. He then rises to a standing position. Tell young children they are now a flower or tree, growing upward. This is the most stable way to rise.

Alternate to Step Two.

Instead of rocking back on her heels, Yuan, above right, braces herself with one bent leg as she rises. This position is not as stable as Jamal's, but will work if you lack the strength to rise from a squatting position. Yuan finds it easier to brace herself with her fists rather than with her outstretched hands. If you still have

Look! I got up!

trouble rising, try bracing your hands on one knee as you rise, although this may decrease stability even further.

Chapter Two Checklist of Skills

❏ I can do the T-Position (Safety Lock)

❏ I can do the V-Position

❏ I can do the Reverse V-Position

❏ I can fall down as safely as possible

❏ I can get back up

❏ I can do a Drop-and-Roll off skates

❏ I can remain standing on the rink floor without falling

❏ I can pick up one foot, and then the other, without falling

Notes

_____

_____

_____

_____

_____

_____

_____

_____

_____

_____

_____

Chapter Three: Start Skating

A Few Tips to Remember

One. As you begin to skate, remember to "skate intentionally". A swimmer uses not only her arms, but every limb, every muscle and every movement to help her swim well. It's no different with skating. Skate with your whole body, not just your lower half. Avoid what I call the "dangling arms syndrome".

Two. Great posture for beginning skaters means head over shoulders, shoulders over hips and hips over heels. Imagine a pole going from the sky, through your head and all the way down through your heels to the ground.

Three. I can't say this enough. Don't forget to bend your knees. Your knees are your body's shock absorbers. Straight "matchstick legs" go down, and they go down hard. Bend your knees.

V-Marching

Once you are able to stand up on the floor in your skates and remain standing, you are ready to skate. The first kind of skating is called "V-marching". V-marching is the same in quad skates, inline skates and even ice skates. It's called V-marching and not V-walking because when you walk, your heel hits the floor first, followed by the ball of your foot and then your toes; but when you march, your entire foot meets the floor.

Get on the skate floor. If there is a step down to the floor, the safest way to get there is to crawl out on your hands and knees and then get up. Remember to place your feet in the Safety Lock position after you rise. In many rinks, there is no step down, and the floor is surrounded with a carpeted wall. **I discourage students from hanging onto walls, railings or "skate mates" unless they can't progress any other way.**

We begin to skate with tiny marching steps. Assume the V-position. Remember that your toes don't need to be pointed outward very far, no more than 45 degrees. Keep your back straight, your eyes looking straight ahead, and your knees bent a little. Extend your arms to waist level.

Lift up your right leg and take a small marching step – a baby step. Put your right leg down. Lift up your left leg and take another small step. Make sure your feet stay in the V-position as you take each step. And keep your skates from knocking into each other. Even a little tap can make you fall.

You are not trying to glide yet as you concentrate on these little steps. However, as you gain practice, you will notice that you slowly begin to roll as you step. **It's the act of one angled foot pushing against the other that makes you go.** If you try to skate in the Piano Keys Position, that is, with your feet parallel, you will find it hard to get anywhere because neither skate has anything to push against. I call this unfortunate situation "*Parallelitis*", and I see it in kids all the time.

At the other extreme, if your toes are pointing outward in a greater than 45 degree angle, your skates may begin to roll away from each other, causing you to lose your balance or even end up in an unintended split – which, I can tell you from experience, is not fun.

If you forget this essential V-position, think of the clown feet below and maybe you'll remember. If you still have trouble keeping your feet in the V-position, practice at home, off skates. Eventually, it will feel natural.

Clown Feet

What to Do When the Student Cannot Remain Standing

Sometimes a student, either through fear or low muscle tone or other reasons, simply cannot remain standing. Even the smallest sensation of rolling sends this person flying, and she can become extremely discouraged. Here's what to do:

Check all eight wheels on the student's skates. If they are rolling freely, have the rink tighten them uniformly so that they turn noticeably *less* freely. This resistance hampering the rotation of the wheels creates a different skating experience. Hopefully, the student will soon start to feel a bit more in control. Later, after she is able to stand without falling and to make short V-marches, you can gradually begin to loosen the wheels again.

For a student who is really and truly too terrified to progress, the rink can temporarily tighten the wheels so much that they *lock,* or refuse to turn at all. As the student begins to relax and make a little progress, you can gradually loosen them again.

What Happens When You Skate?

The diagram on the following page shows what is really happening when you begin to take those tiny V-marches, and those tiny marches start to turn into tiny rolls. Remember, the closer your push-offs are to the vertical dotted line in the diagram, the more efficient your skating will be.

43

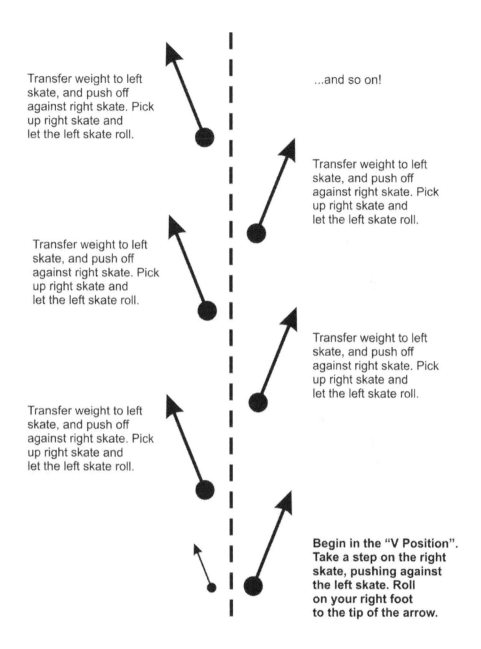

Transfer weight to left skate, and push off against right skate. Pick up right skate and let the left skate roll.

...and so on!

Transfer weight to left skate, and push off against right skate. Pick up right skate and let the left skate roll.

Transfer weight to left skate, and push off against right skate. Pick up right skate and let the left skate roll.

Transfer weight to left skate, and push off against right skate. Pick up right skate and let the left skate roll.

Transfer weight to left skate, and push off against right skate. Pick up right skate and let the left skate roll.

Begin in the "V Position". Take a step on the right skate, pushing against the left skate. Roll on your right foot to the tip of the arrow.

Follow the Chart from the Bottom

As you can see, you're not skating in a straight line so much as weaving back and forth across it. In fact, if you fix your eyes on a spot on the opposite wall as you skate, you will see that it appears to move slightly to the left and right as you move.

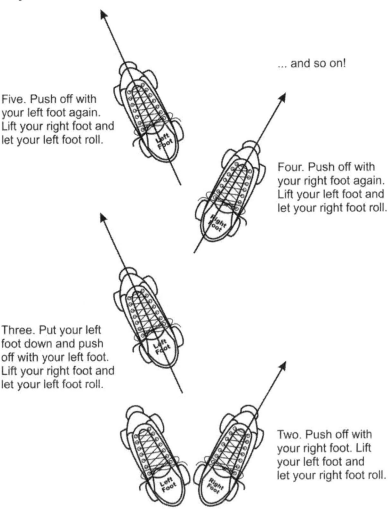

... and so on!

Five. Push off with your left foot again. Lift your right foot and let your left foot roll.

Four. Push off with your right foot again. Lift your left foot and let your right foot roll.

Three. Put your left foot down and push off with your left foot. Lift your right foot and let your left foot roll.

Two. Push off with your right foot. Lift your left foot and let your right foot roll.

One. Assume the "V Position". Your weight will be evenly distributed on both feet.

Chapter Three Checklist of Skills

☐   I keep my knees a little bent and my back straight

☐   I can do small V-Marches

☐   I can do small V-Rolls (skate-march with beginning glide)

Notes

_____

_____

_____

_____

_____

_____

_____

_____

_____

_____

_____

_____

_____

_____

_____

_____

_____

_____

_____

Chapter Four: Skate Well

Edges

If you stick with skating long enough, and particularly if you begin artistic or speed training, you'll start hearing the term "edges". What are edges? In the singular, an edge is simply the side of either skate – inner or outer – which bears, or should bear, more of your weight as you skate. Even V-glides and T-starts use edges; however, edges become more important when skating around a curve. The edges needed depend on the move you're executing, the direction you're going (forward or backwards), and the foot you're using.

There are four possible edges: left outside, left inside, right inside, and right outside. Edges look a little different on quad vs. inline skates. Shown on the next page and viewed from the back is a pair of quad skates. Each set of two wheels is labeled with its corresponding edge.

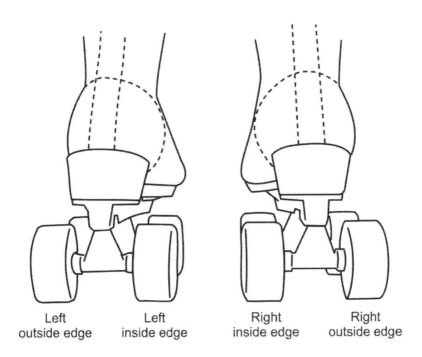

| Left outside edge | Left inside edge | Right inside edge | Right outside edge |

In quad skating, the inner or outer wheels themselves don't normally tilt when the skater goes around a curve. Rather, the weight placed on the wheels by the skater's body forces the skate to go in the direction indicated by the edge (helped or hindered by the presence of loosened trucks or the lack of them).

In inline skating, the wheels are slim and lined up one behind another, and there are no trucks. Therefore, the wheels themselves have to tilt to form the edge.

In the illustration below, we'll take another look at Wimbledon Wimpleton III, as he navigates a curve in Saturday's speed meet.

Inside edge of the right skate's wheels

Outside edge of the left skate's wheels

In order to get around the curve as efficiently as possible, Wimbledon creates an edge with both the inside edge of his right wheels and the outside edge of his left wheels. The angle of his legs and feet causes the wheels themselves to tilt.

Why Worry About Edges?

It's true that as a beginning recreational skater, you don't need to overly concern yourself with edges as would, for example, an aspiring figure skater. Even though that's true, understanding how edges are used will improve your skating. And some of the basic beginning moves, such as crossovers and carving, do make use of them.

If your rink has figure circles or any other marked curved lines, use them. Practice skating on each foot around a circle or curve, first in one direction and then the other. When you veer off course, as you probably will at first, correct your path with gentle push-offs from the other foot. As ice skaters will tell you, tracing figures is not terribly exciting, but I guarantee that figures will improve your skating no matter where you decide to take it.

Back to Quad Skates:
The Relationship Between Trucks and Edges

If you have quad skates, pick one up. Try to wiggle the front and back sets of wheels on their respective axles. If there is some give, that means that your trucks have been loosened.

Only the least expensive quad skates have axles which are welded to the plate and cannot be loosened, eliminating the need for trucks. In my opinion, that kind of skate is for young kids only.

Remember Ashanti? Let's look at her on another day as she cannonballs around a corner. Her feet are in the parallel "Piano Keys" position. Her dad, who loves to rhythm skate, decided to loosen her trucks. Study the angle of Ashanti's wheels opposed to the angle of her boots. It's somewhat over 90 degrees. Ashanti is leaning to her right which forces more of her weight onto her right outside edge and her left inside edge. Using these edges helps her get around that corner more smoothly.

Even if her trucks were not loosened, she would still lean on her right outside edge and her left inside edge. However, she would find it a bit more difficult to navigate the curve. Ashanti's dad would be the first to tell you that looser trucks require greater skill. For that reason, I recommend loosening trucks very gradually, just a little bit every few weeks. Skill is not something you get overnight; it only comes with practice.

The T-Start: A More Powerful Push-off For Faster Skating

When you get the "V-march" down, you'll be ready to skate a little faster. This medium-paced skating motion is called "stroking". It's done the same way with both quad skates and inlines. Begin with what's called a "T-Start". Remember the Safety Lock Position? The T-Start, seen below, looks just like it, except that the back skate is a bit further from the front skate. You can push off from either foot, though the illustration below shows the right foot leading.

The T-Start

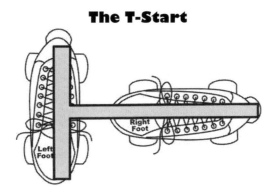

For most people, one leg is dominant, that is, somewhat stronger than the other. For some it's the right leg, for others, the left. In the illustration, the right leg is dominant, and the left foot braces you for take-off. **Each leg must be able to bear your entire body weight for a second or two as you stroke along.** And your knees should be bent. Ready, set, go.

Below is Austin again – something's different about him today, can't quite put my finger on it. Anyway, Austin began with a strong T-start and is now skating at a medium pace. He is just beginning a new left stroke. See how he still gazes ahead, but his knees are more deeply bent. You can't see it as well from the front, but his hips are bent forward by the same angle as his knees (see page 56 for a side view). Later, at his right leg's maximum extension, his hips will be over his ankles. His chin will be over his left knee which will be over his toes. I call this position "Chimney Toes", not because it's accurate, but because it's funny and helps me remember the formation.

As Austin begins each stroke, his opposite foot pushes out, not back, but to the side. He doesn't let his loose foot trail behind him, which not only helps him avoid toe blisters from incorrect push-offs, but makes his skating more effic- ient. His back is pretty flat. His weight is now more on his heels than on his entire foot or toes. He pumps his arms, not only

for balance, but to help him gain even more momentum. I hear Austin is thinking about joining the speed team.

Good Posture Versus Poor Posture

Now that you are going a little faster, let's talk more about posture. Good posture will help your skating, and poor posture will hinder it. The following illustration depicts another skater, Taylor. Oh, my.

Taylor hasn't been skating for very long, and he's not nearly as comfortable on his skates as Austin. Look at Taylor lurching forward as he skates. His back, neck, and shoulders are hunched. He's looking down and his knees are straight and locked. His arms are extended, not out but forward.

Do you see how, in a misguided effort to keep from falling, Taylor has thrown his entire body off balance? Doesn't he look like he's about to tip over? That's because he is. I see people skate like this all the time. I call it the "Frankenstein Posture". It seems to be a natural defensive measure, but it doesn't work very well, and Taylor is not enjoying his skating.

Let's look at Taylor again, after he's had some lessons. In the picture at left, Taylor's posture has improved. His head is over his shoulders. His shoulders are over his hips. His hips are over his heels. That dotted line going through him proves it. And his knees are bent. He is looking straight ahead and not down. He is not having to work as hard as before – his wheels are doing their share of the work. The only thing I would like Taylor to do is put that I-pod in his pocket so that his hand is free. And maybe start working on building up a little speed. Taylor? *Taylor?*

Never mind. Let's fast-forward to six months later. Taylor still hasn't changed his clothes, but he *is* going faster. His hips and knees are both bent at the same 90 degree angle, and his back is flat. He used to carry his weight over his toes, but now it is more over his heels. He's got the chin-over-knee-over-toes idea down. And he ditched the I-pod.

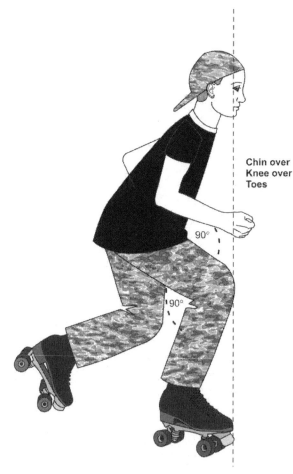

Chin over
Knee over
Toes

90°

90°

The only thing he's doing wrong now is allowing his left foot to trail behind him a bit. He's going to have some blisters from all those toe push-offs. His free foot should be extended to his side as he strokes.

Distance Between Skates

Another type of poor skating posture involves the distance between skates during stroking. Look at Katrina (right). Her back is nice and straight – but notice how far apart her feet are. Katrina needs to draw in her skates as she starts each stroke, to no wider than shoulder width. She imagines that this wider posture steadies her, but it is actually making her work harder than she needs to,

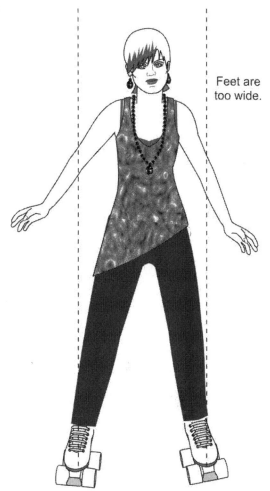

Feet are too wide.

not to mention increasing her chances of losing her balance. This is another example of a beginner's natural defensive mechanism which only makes things worse. Usually I see kids skating with their feet too far apart, but now and then I see it in adults as well.

Below is Katrina again, after a bit more practice. Now her feet are closer together and she is skating more efficiently.

Feet are shoulder-width. Good job!

Arms Should Help, Not Hinder

One thing I like about Katrina's improved posture at left is her arms. They are not flailing wildly like those of many beginning students. Instead, each arm is a controlled mirror image of the other one, and extended to waist level.

Katrina is now skating intentionally. Her arm movements are helping keep her balance, instead of making her even more unstable. Different skating disciplines (artistic, jam, speed, derby, etc.) have different ways in which the arms are employed, but every beginning skater needs to learn basic limb control and balance. Arms should help, not hinder.

Four Ways to Stop

Since you're skating faster now, it might be helpful to know how to stop. There are lots of ways. Here are three of them that are useful for beginners, and another that you'll enjoy when you're a little more advanced.

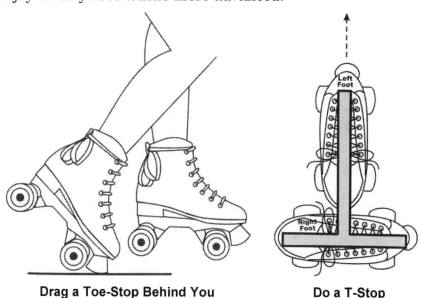

Drag a Toe-Stop Behind You   **Do a T-Stop**

Use Your Toe-Stop

As you skate, firmly drag the rubber toe-stop of one skate behind the other skate. The friction will slow you down and bring you to a stop. A plastic toe-stop will bring you to a more gradual stop. If you are wearing inlines, your brake is probably in the back. In that case, lift up your toe and drag the back brake behind you. The inline brake is plastic and will not bring you to an abrupt stop.

Do a "T-Stop"

Remember the "T-Start"? You can come to a stop using the same position. While you are skating, center one skate behind the other at a right angle, in the shape of an upside-down capital "T". Now drag all of the wheels of the second skate firmly behind you. This will bring you to an effective stop. T-stopping more gently is a good way to slow down without stopping.

Some new skaters find the idea of swinging one foot firmly behind the other at that right angle to be unnerving. If this is true of you, it may help to practice the movement either off skates, or in the center of the rink in a stationary position. See the drill on page 84.

Snowplow

The snowplow is discussed in the section on swizzling.

Spin-Stop

The spin-stop is discussed in the section on spinning.

One-Foot Glide

It's important that each leg is able to bear your entire body weight for short lengths of time. As you make a stroke with your left leg, swing your right leg behind you. Raise your right foot three inches off the floor for a few seconds. At the same time, extend your arms to the height of your waist, arch your back slightly, point your right toe, and look straight ahead and not down. Practice on the other foot. Over time, your legs will become so strong, and your balance so fine, that you will be able to glide on either foot for a considerable length of time.

To the right is Golda, practicing her one-foot glide. Wow, look at her below. Her one-foot glide has turned into a beautiful spiral, a classic figure skating move. Skating spirals are based on the arabesque move in ballet. They can be done forward or backwards, along a straight line or a curve, and along any skating edge.

How to Swizzle

Swizzles are also known as scissors. Swizzling is a great way to get around without having to lift either foot. You can swizzle forward or backwards. Swizzling also provides a way to come to a natural, comfortable stop.

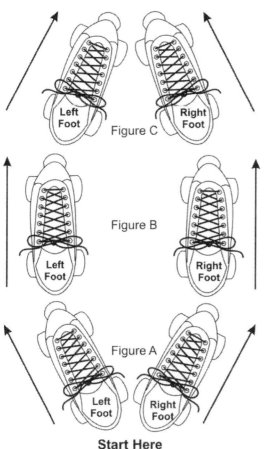

Figure C

Figure B

Figure A

Start Here

To swizzle, place your feet in the V-position (Figure A to the left). Keep your weight evenly distributed over both feet, but with more of your weight on your heels than on your toes. Your heels will power your swizzling, and your toes will steer it. Push off with both feet simultaneously. Each angled foot will provide leverage for the other foot.

Your feet will roll outward. Skate outward until your feet are no more than a foot to a foot-and-a-half apart (Figure B above).

Now steer both skates into a parallel alignment. With your weight still on your heels, point your toes inward. Use your toes to steer your skates back in. The completed move looks like an oval shape, and concludes with you in a Reverse V-position (Figure C on the previous page). The illustration below shows these positions from the front.

Start Here

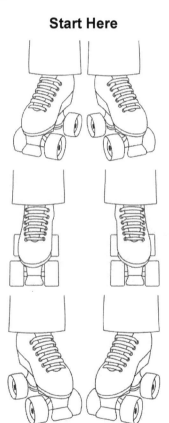

Repeat the motion. Each time you begin, your toes will be pointed outward, and each time you end, your toes will be pointed inward. With your weight on your heels, steer your toes back outward and begin a new swizzle. The left section of the chart on the next page shows a forward swizzle.

Two Ways to Start Skating Backwards
Reverse Swizzle

Start with your feet in the Reverse V-position. This time you will steer with your heels and power with your toes. Slowly swizzle backwards. Midway through the maneuver, make your feet parallel, and then draw them closed to the V-position. Refer to the "Backwards Swizzling" chart on the next page. Remember to keep your back straight and knees bent, and try not to look down.

Reverse V-March

Place your feet in the Reverse V-position. Instead of swizzling, begin a slow backwards march. Hold the Reverse V-position as you lift one foot and then the other. As with forward V-marching, the march soon becomes a glide.

Coming to a Stop Via Plowstop

The easiest, most basic way to stop with any type of backwards skating is to lean forward and drag your front toe stops. If you are swizzling slowly, however, whether forward or backwards, you can come to a slow, natural stop without using your toe stops. Ending a forward swizzle in a stop is called a plowstop, or snowplow.

Patterns for Forward and Reverse Swizzling

The two charts below show the patterns of both a more lengthy forward swizzle, and a backwards swizzle.

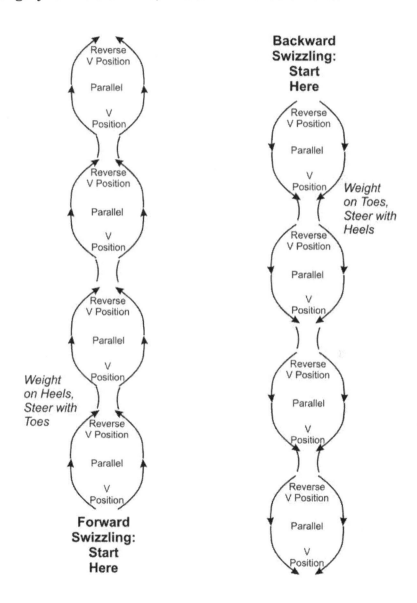

Half-Swizzle

Now that you can swizzle, the "Half-Swizzle" should be a piece of cake. In this move, only one foot swizzles. The swizzling foot propels your other leg which bears most of your weight as it rolls forward.

Grapevine

You can also add other elements to swizzling. To grapevine, instead of ending each forward swizzle in a Reverse V-position, steer your right foot further forward, to the front of your left foot, and then draw it back (Figure B). You do not need to raise your foot. From there, steer your left foot in front of the right foot, and so on. In grapevining, most of your weight will always be on the foot which is not crossing in front of the other one.

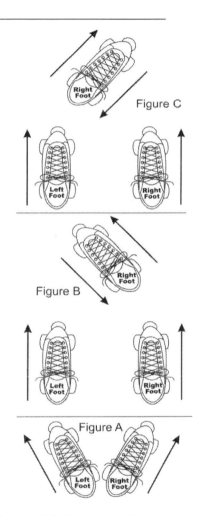

Figure C

Figure B

Figure A

Grapevining is not hard to do, and it looks cool.

Three Ways to Skate Around a Corner
Carving

The first and easiest way is called "carving", or "parallel turns". Let's look at Courtney as she carves in a counterclockwise direction. First, she gathers momentum. Then she stops stroking, rolling on both skates with her skates parallel. She rotates her head, shoulders and waist toward the left. Her ankles also lean slightly to the left. Her weight creates a left outside edge and a right inside edge. All of these combined movements steer Courtney toward the left. If she was going faster, she would need to bend her knees more, the inside knee a little more than the outside. Oh – and do you see how the angle between Courtney's wheels and boots is different? That's because the trucks on her skates have been loosened. If she was wearing  inlines, the wheels themselves would provide the angles. The only thing I would like Courtney to do is to bend her knees more. And smile already.

(Check out the useful carving drills on page 83.)

Pumping

The second way to turn a corner is by repeated push-offs from one leg, or "pumping". This move is a lot like riding a child's manual scooter. Say that you want to turn in a counterclockwise direction. Pretend that your left skate is the base of the imaginary scooter in the illustration below. Like Keenan, you will push off repeatedly with your right foot.

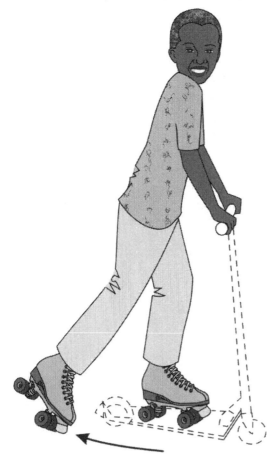

For leverage, place your right skate at a 30 degree angle to your left skate. Your left skate will roll around the corner on its left outside edge, as your right skate provides continuous push offs. If you wish to turn in a clockwise direction, switch feet.

This maneuver also works well as a strength-building drill (see pages 82 and 83).

Crossovers

The third way of turning is with right crossovers. Many beginning students find crossovers difficult until their legs and ankles are stronger and their balance more stable. It is helpful to first practice the technique off skates.

To the left is Courtney again. She begins with a stroke of her left leg, with most of her body weight on her left skate. With knees bent, she swings her right leg cleanly over her left knee and plants it to the forward/left of her left foot. While this is happening, her head, shoulders and waist have turned slightly toward the left, with her right shoulder over her left knee. As her right skate touches the floor, she transfers all of her weight from her left leg back to her right leg, and swings her left leg into position again. The crossovers plus her body rotation are making her turn. If she was on inline skates, the wheels and not the trucks would be forming the angles.

Look! She's smiling today.

Chapter Four Skills Checklist

☐ I can do a T-Start

☐ I can stroke (a longer glide with stronger push-offs)

☐ My back is not hunched over as I skate

☐ I look straight ahead while I skate, not down

☐ I bend my knees slightly while skating

☐ I bring my skates in to shoulder width while stroking

☐ My arm movements are controlled and purposeful

☐ I can stop by using my toe-stop

☐ I can stop by using a T-Stop

☐ I can swizzle frontwards

☐ I can do a snowplow stop

☐ I can swizzle backwards

☐ I can skate backwards using a Reverse V-march

☐ I can do a half-swizzle

☐ I can grapevine

☐ I can carve (parallel turns)

☐ I can pump in a forward direction, on either leg

☐ I can do brief, one-foot glides

☐ I can do right forward crossovers

Notes

_____

_____

_____

Chapter Five: Become an Intermediate Skater

Five Tips for Improvement

In this chapter, you will venture into the world of intermediate skating. Below are five general tips that will help you greatly.

One. Think about every movement. Where are your feet? Which foot is bearing more of your weight, and on what part of the skate? What are your arms doing? Is your posture correct? If you are going fast, are your hip angles and knee angles identical? Where are you looking? And so on.

Two. In the periods between skating sessions, visualize yourself skating far beyond your current ability. For example, if you want to learn the two-footed spin, imagine yourself doing it perfectly, and looking great. Sooner or later, your real skills will catch up.

Three. Watch tutorials on YouTube detailing the moves you are trying to learn. Ice skating tutorials can be particularly helpful, because many of the moves are transferrable to roller skates, and the standards for excellence sometimes seem to be higher. There are also many great tutorials made by roller skaters of all stripes. Use the "pause" button frequently to further examine what is happening. Keep in mind, of course, that some of the people making the videos are hobby skaters and may not give you the most accurate information.

Four. Make short videos of yourself skating. As you view the videos with a critical eye, you are likely to spot problems right away. "Oh!" you might exclaim. "I didn't realize my left foot is pronating!" Or, "Yikes, look at me slouching!" Seeing yourself on video can be a humbling experience, but is guaranteed to make you a better skater.

Five. Almost every skater has a stronger leg and a weaker leg. Don't get lazy and always rely on the dominant leg. Force yourself to do the same moves with the weaker leg. For example, I find it easier to turn from front to back in a counterclockwise direction, and to turn back around in a clockwise direction. One way feels natural, and the other way feels awkward. By forcing myself to do it both ways, I strengthen myself as a skater.

Two-footed Spins

How to Spin from a Stationary Position

Skaters usually prefer to spin in one direction or another, but to avoid confusion, all of the spins in this section will be counterclockwise. Stand in the center of the rink with your feet in a wide V-position. Your heels should be 6-12 inches apart and your skates should form at least a 90 degree angle. In order to spin in a counterclockwise direction, you are first going to "wind yourself up" in a *clockwise* direction.

You can get the hang of this with some exaggerated movements. First, twist your head, shoulders, arms and waist to the right, until the angle between your shoulders and your skates is around 90 degrees. This will give you the power you need to spin in the opposite direction. Now forcefully twist your head, shoulders, arms and waist in a counterclockwise direction. When you do, your skates will follow the rest of your body's lead and begin to roll.

You may have started the spin with more of your weight on your right foot, but now try to distribute your weight over both feet. Keep your skates firmly in that wide V-position. Tell your legs and feet they are made of steel and cannot change positions. Your wheels are tracing a semicircular path for you to follow. If your feet move out of position, the path is broken and you are likely to fall.

Let's look at this aerial view of Emiko below, as she prepares for a counterclockwise, two-footed spin. Emiko has placed her feet in a wide V-position. Her arms are extended and she has started to "wind" her body in a clockwise direction. She continues to wind herself up for the spin. Now she is just about ready to let it rip.

Top two reason spinners fall:

1) posture is not erect.

2) feet do not maintain the V-position.

Once you are able to spin for one full rotation, you can experiment with small or wide spins. Keeping your arms out while spinning will slow the spin. Tucking your arms in will make you spin faster. If you want to spin longer, spin on one toe and one heel. For a really wide spin, lean inward.

How to Spin from a Rolling Position

Next, we'll learn how to launch into a spin preceded by a forward roll. Say you are stroking along and wish to spin in a counterclockwise direction. You don't need to "wind yourself up" to the extent that you did from the stationary position. That's because your spin will be powered by the momentum you've already built up through your forward strokes.

Push off with your right skate, which initially will steer your spin. Firmly plant your left foot into that wide V-position of 90 degrees or greater. Don't forget to also turn your head, shoulders and waist to the left. Enter the spin, being careful to maintain your wheels' firm semicircular path. Keep spinning with your weight distributed over both skates.

Spin-Stop

Another of the many ways to come to a stop is to end a forward stroke in a spin. First build up a little speed. Then push off with your right foot and launch into the spin.

Try it, it's fun.

How to Turn from Front to Back

TIP: The following principle applies to every type of turn and rotation. Every time you turn from front to back, or from back to front, make sure that your head turns first – after that, your shoulders, waist, and on down to your feet. (This will all happen within a second or so.) This progression stabilizes your turns. Turn your head first, and your feet will follow. Just like a dancer, make sure to involve your whole body as you make each turn, and your life as a skater will be more fun.

Groundwork – the Spread Eagle

While you are skating forward, transfer your weight to your right skate. Rotate your left skate until it is at a 180 degree angle to your right skate – heel to heel and with toes pointed in opposite directions. Make sure your weight is distributed between both skates as you continue to roll.

In the illustration on the next page, Ken has mastered the spread eagle. If he would just stop staring at Katrina, he could learn how to turn that spread eagle into a beautiful Mohawk turn.

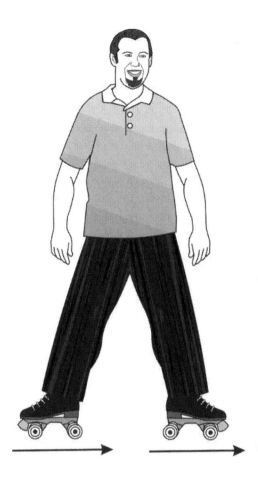

The Mohawk Turn

Not everyone is flexible enough to force their legs into a heel-to-heel spread eagle position like Ken. If you are one of these, see the "Modified Mohawk" section on the next page. But if you aren't, you can use that spread eagle to easily complete a backwards turn. To turn in a counterclockwise direction from a spread eagle, first turn your head left. In the next instant, transfer your weight from your right skate, which was rolling forward, to your left skate, which was also rolling forward but is now facing backward. Bring the right skate around by the front wheel or wheels, until it is parallel with the left skate. Put all the wheels of the right skate on the ground and continue to skate backwards. You have completed a Mohawk.

To complete the circle and turn back around, turn your head to the left, then rotate your left leg until you are again rolling in a spread eagle. Pick up your right skate and bring it around until it is parallel with the left skate. You are going forward again.

Modified Mohawk Turn

The modified Mohawk is just like the Mohawk except that there is no spread eagle. To execute a modified Mohawk in a counterclockwise direction, first push off on your right skate. Gently veer left on the skate's inside edge. Bring the heel of your left skate close in to form a 90 degree-or-greater angle, as wide as you can make it. Transfer your weight to your left skate which will now be travelling backwards; you can either pick up the right skate and bring it around, or bring it around by the front wheel or wheels.

Travelling backwards, make one reverse V-glide to switch feet. The illustration on the next page will show you how to turn back around, completing a full circle.

Start Here

Glide backwards on your right foot. Veer right by using a right outside edge. To make the edge, extend your left foot behind you and lean your body to the right. Experiment with the degree of curve.

To go forward again, rotate your left foot 90 degrees to the left. Transfer your weight to your left foot. Glide using a left outside edge. Now your right foot will be behind you.

In the modified Mohawk turn, the path of your skating changes somewhat, which can make your skating more interesting to look at. If the move seems really hard at first, practice it off skates. Remember to let not just your legs, but your head and body assist you with the turns.

Spin-Turn

Transform a half-spin into a backwards turn. Skating forward, enter into a counterclockwise, two-footed spin. Only complete a half-circle, which will leave you facing backwards. To turn back around, complete the spin.

Chapter Five Skills Checklist

☐ I can do a two-footed spin from a standing position

☐ I can do a two-footed spin from a rolling position

☐ I can do a spread eagle

☐ I can do a Mohawk and/or a modified Mohawk turn

☐ I can turn from front to back using a half-spin

☐ I can stop by going into a spin

☐ I can turn back around

Notes

_____

_____

_____

_____

_____

_____

_____

_____

_____

_____

_____

_____

_____

Chapter Six: Get Stronger

Two General Tips

One. Skate as often as you can. Skating once a month will not help you improve much. Skating once a week may not be enough, either. The more frequently you skate, the better you will get. I know it's not always possible, but try to skate at least twice per week, for at least two hours per session. If you can't get to a rink, try inline skating outdoors.

Two. Don't forget to stretch. Stretching your quadriceps, calves and hamstrings before skating can improve your performance. Neglecting to stretch can increase your chances of stiffness and even injury.

Drills for Skaters on Skates

Without strong legs, ankles and feet, and knees that are able to bend, skating can be frustrating, not to mention more dangerous. Below are some drills and exercises to strengthen your thighs, calves and feet. I use all of these in my classes.

Pumping (Scootering)

You have already seen this exercise on page 68. Pumping gets you used to balancing all of your weight on one leg. Pump on one leg for a lap or two, then switch. You can also turn this exercise into a race between students. You can even have students remove their back skate as they pump.

Side-step or Crab Walk

Assume a slight Reverse V-position, only a 10 or 20 degree angle. Your back should be straight and your knees bent a bit. Step sideways to the right about ten steps. Don't allow yourself to roll. Now step back to the left ten steps. Now step side to side. Do it to music if you can. This exercise will give you better control of your movements.

Back Skate Raise

Assume a V-position. With knees slightly bent, raise each skate *behind* you a few inches for a second or two.

Play Ball!

Just plain fun and helps more than anyone would suspect. See page 26 for details.

Alternating Left and Right Crossovers

While skating in a straight line (not around corners), perform a right crossover. Alternate legs and perform a left crossover. Right, then left again. (Crossovers will probably be easier for one leg than the other.)

Rolling Squats or Cannonballs

Tuck in your arms. Lower your body as far down to the floor as you can, and swizzle or stroke. You can hug your knees or extend your arms. This exercise improves your balance and strengthens your thighs. (See Fig. C on page 34.)

Shoot the Duck

From a rolling squat, extend one leg forward, and roll.

Hopping

Practice hopping on skates. Hop forward, or hop from side to side. Don't hop backwards just yet. Keep your weight on all wheels.

Carving Between or Around Cones

Set up six to eight cones in a line in the middle of the skate floor. Place them about two yards apart. Weave around the cones from left to right, trying not to hit any of them. As you improve, place the cones closer together. You can also carve, or circle, around one cone. How close can you get to the center cone?

Rocking Horse

The Rocking Horse is one swizzle forwards, followed by one swizzle backwards. Repeat twenty times.

T-Position Drill

Assume the Piano Keys Parallel position. Swing one foot in back of the other foot to form the T-position. Bring the foot back to the Parallel position. Repeat ten times on each foot.

T-Start Rolling Race

For two or more students. Push off from a T-position and go directly into either a two-footed or a one-footed roll. How far can you roll?

V-Position to Reverse V-Position Pivot

Assume the V-position. Rise on one toe and one heel. Pivot to the right on the raised heel and toe into the Reverse V-Position, then back into the V-position. Repeat twenty times. Rise on the opposite toe and heel, and repeat.

Backwards Wiggle

Assume the Piano Keys position. Extend your arms in front of you, crossing one hand over the other. Raising your heels slightly as you go, pivot on both toes 25 or 30 degrees, in the same direction and at the same time. Land on your heels after the pivot. Then pivot in the opposite direction. Thrust your hip sideways with each pivot to strengthen and stabilize the move. Once you've gotten the movement down, see if you can pivot/wiggle backwards.

Exercises to Practice at Home or Before Skating

Below are some additional exercises which will stretch and strengthen your skating muscles, including your back.

Calf Stretch

To stretch your calves, put both feet flat on the ground, either side by side or with one foot in front of the other. Make sure toes are pointing forward. Brace your hands against a wall and lean forward gently, bending at the elbows.

Hamstring Stretch

Sit down with your legs stretched in front of you. Bend forward gently at the waist and touch your toes.

The Dancer Pose

This yoga move is great for skaters. Sarah, on the next page, begins by balancing on her left foot. She grasps her right inside ankle with her right hand. She pulls it as far back, and up, as she can. She extends her left arm above her head. She arches her back and looks up. She holds the pose for as long as she can on each foot.

If balancing is a challenge, try bracing one hand against a wall. This exercise improves overall balance and strength, and also stretches the quadriceps (big thigh muscles).

Toe Raises

Toe raises increase strength in your feet and ankles. Take off your shoes. Stand up and balance on your toes. Raise and lower your toes thirty times.

Squats or Deep Knee Bends

Hold your arms straight out in front of you. Keeping your back straight, bend your knees and lower yourself as far as you can go. Slowly raise yourself back up. Repeat ten times. You can also do this against a wall. Keep your back flat against the wall and lower yourself until your thighs and calves form a 90 degree angle. Rise and repeat.

Other Sports

Regular walking, jogging, biking, jumping on a trampoline, martial arts, dance... engaging in just about any sport on a regular basis will make you a stronger skater.

> **A sedentary lifestyle accompanied by poor dietary habits can make skating more difficult, while general fitness will make it easier and more fun.**

"Ow, It Hurts!"
Some Common Sources of Pain

Sometimes a beginning skater will experience minor or even acute pain while skating. Below is a list of symptoms, possible causes, and cures. If in doubt, consult your doctor.

Symptom: **Lower backache while skating.**
Possible causes: Poor general physical fitness; or a medical problem.
What to do: Incrcase activity level with walking, sit-ups, and stretching; consult doctor.

Symptom: **Aching or hurting feet.**
Possible causes: Skates fit poorly or are cutting into skin; structural foot abnormalities (see page 19).
What to do: Adjust or exchange skates; use orthotics; perform exercises for pronating or supinating feet.

Symptom: **Out of breath from only a few minutes of skating.**
Possible cause: Poor general fitness; heart or lung problems.
What to do: Increase activity level; consult a doctor.

Symptom: **Shin splints in front of calf.**

Possible causes: Increasing activity level too quickly; pronating or supinating feet (see page 19); poor skating form, i.e., too much weight on either the heels or toes; sudden starts and stops with twisting of the legs; poorly fitting skates.

What to do: Don't exercise for a few days and let your muscles rest; insert orthotics in skates; try different skates.

Symptom: **Other leg pain.**

Possible causes: Your muscles could be stiff.

What to do: Stretch your calves, hamstrings and quadriceps before skating. Avoid dehydration.

Symptom: **Trembling ankles.**

Possible causes: You are not used to skating.

What to do: Give it some time. Your ankles will get stronger.

Symptom: **Blisters.**

Possible causes: Skates don't fit well. Or, you are pushing off too much on your toes.

What to do: Replace skates if necessary. Mark the spot where blisters occur, and apply duct tape over skin before the next skate. Learn the correct way to push off.

Suggested Sequence for a Four- to Six-Week Skating Course

Week One

☐ Talk about safety and general fitness.

☐ Off skates, teach the Safety Lock and V-positions.

☐ Off skates, demonstrate and practice regular walking vs. skate-marching.

☐ Off skates, demonstrate and practice how to fall and get up.

☐ Have student V-march from one wall to the other in her socks.

☐ On skates, have student practice standing, or gently bouncing from knee to knee, without falling.

☐ Have student practice small V-marches on skates.

☐ Skate Exercises: the Dancer Pose, leg stretches.

Week Two

☐ Off skates, demonstrate stopping with rubber stopper.

☐ Demonstrate the T-stop.

☐ On skates, have the student practice V-marches and stopping, through games like "Freeze" and "Red Light, Green Light". Keep practicing the skate-marches.

☐ Off Skate Exercises: Squats and Toe Raises.

Week Three

☐ Off skates, demonstrate the motion of skates going faster, with a stronger push-off from the T-Start position. (You can hold a pair of skates in front of you to demonstrate.)

☐ Demonstrate the Drop and Roll and the Cannonball.

☐ Practice skating. Practice side-stepping.

☐ Race: Have several students remove one skate. Have them push off repeatedly with the skateless foot, and roll with the remaining skate.

Weeks Four - Six

☐ Swizzling, frontwards and backwards.

☐ Snowplow stop.

☐ Carving, pumping, crossovers. Variations of swizzle.

☐ Spread eagle, Mohawk, Modified Mohawk, Spin-turn. Practice everything.

Complete Checklist of Skills

☐ I can do the Safety-lock position
☐ I can do the V-position
☐ I can do the Reverse V-position
☐ I can fall down properly
☐ I can get back up
☐ I can do a drop and roll
☐ I can do a rolling cannonball
☐ I can stay standing on the rink floor without falling
☐ I can do a V-march
☐ I can do a V-Roll (skate-march with beginning glide)
☐ I can do a T-Start
☐ I can stroke (a longer glide with stronger push-offs)
☐ I can do a one-foot glide
☐ I have good posture when I skate
☐ I bend my knees slightly while skating
☐ I bring my skates in to shoulder width while stroking
☐ My arm movements are controlled and purposeful
☐ I can stop using my toe-stop
☐ I can stop using a T-Stop
☐ I can swizzle frontwards
☐ I can do a snowplow stop
☐ I can swizzle backwards
☐ I can do a half-swizzle
☐ I can grapevine
☐ I can carve (parallel turns)
☐ I can pump on either leg in a forward direction
☐ I can do right forward crossovers
☐ I can do left forward crossovers
☐ I can do a two-footed spin from a standing position
☐ I can do a two-footed spin from a rolling position
☐ I can do a spread eagle
☐ I can do a Mohawk and/or a modified Mohawk turn
☐ I can turn from front to back using a half-spin
☐ I can stop by going into a spin
☐ I can turn back around

Epilogue:
"I Love Skating! What Next?"

I Can Skate! Where Do I Go From Here?

Once you or your student have mastered beginning skating, you may wish to pursue a particular style or branch. Below is a brief overview of each kind of skating.

Artistic or Figure Skating

Artistic or figure skaters perform choreographed dance/ skate routines set to music. (Refer to the illustrations on page 11.) Artistic skaters practice controlled and precise movements, including jumps and spins, for years in order to achieve mastery. They use their arms more than in any other kind of skating, both for balance and for musical expression. Artistic skaters need the larger toe-stops as a starting point for certain kinds of jumps. If you want to learn artistic skating, you should find a professional coach. To find out more about artistic skating, go to www.team-usa.org/USA-Roller-Sports.aspx and click on "Figure". See if there are any artistic skating clubs in your local rinks.

Speed Skating

Speed skating is the sport of racing in skates. You can skate fast in any skates, but to compete as a speed skater, you need special inline skates with oversized wheels. Refer back to the illustrations on page 13. Speed skating is one instance where you do not want your posture erect. Though you should still be looking straight ahead, you should bend forward at the waist, and your knees should be deeply bent. If you want to pursue speed skating, you will need a professional coach. To find out more about speed skating, go to **www.teamusa.org/USA-Roller-Sports.aspx** and click on "Speed Skating". Many rinks have speed coaches and teams.

Jam Skating

Jam skating, a newer style of skating, is a combination of dance, gymnastics including break dancing, and skating. Refer back to the illustrations on page 12. Jam skating can be performed in any kind of skates except speed skates. Most jam skaters wear lightweight quad jam skates with no heel, a low boot, and wide wheels. Larger toe-stops are replaced with smaller stops called jam plugs, or even removed entirely. This is because many jam skating movements are done on the toes, and traditional toe-stops get in the way. To find out more about jam skating, go to **www.wsajamskating.com**.

Roller Derby

Roller derby is a contact sport played by two teams of five members roller skating in the same direction around a track. It has traditionally been all-female, but men's derby is gaining a foothold. To find out more about derby, go to **www.wftda.com**, which is the website for the Women's Flat Track Derby Association.

Roller Hockey

Roller hockey is a form of hockey played on a dry surface using roller skates. There are two styles of roller hockey, one which is played in quad skates and the other played in inlines. To find out more about roller hockey, visit **www.teamusa.org/USA-Roller-Sports.aspx** and click on either "inline hockey" or "rink hockey".

Coloring Pages for Young Skaters

On the following four pages are some coloring pages just for young skaters. You can enlarge and print them out. I hope you enjoy them.

There are many kinds of roller skates.
Can you match these skates with the skaters
who are wearing them?

There are many styles of skating.
Which one do you like best?

"We took skating lessons, and now we can do a safety lock and a cannonball."

"We both like to skate, but there's another sport
we like even better. Can you guess what it is?"

Index